Snakes

Kids Picture Book and Facts about Snakes

Terry Mason

Snakes and the World

Snakes are legless, coldblooded, and carnivorous reptiles belonging to the Animal Kingdom in the suborder Serpentes. They are thought to roam (or crawl) the Earth as early as the Late Cretaceous period, the time when dinosaurs were still alive. Today, there are more than 2,900 species of snakes in the world!

Snakes actually are very interesting creatures. They can be found almost everywhere, whether on land or under the sea. Would you not be curious when you see a real one slithering about?

The Anatomy of a Snake

Snakes have unique bodies. They have flexible and elongated bodies, like a tube. On the outside, they have tough scales, an elastic mouth, a forked tongue for smelling, and rows of teeth. Inside, they have strong bones and muscles to protect their insides and make up for their lack of limbs.

In case you are wondering, snakes do have bones! Snakes are vertebrates – animals that have a backbone and a skeleton. In fact, a snake's backbone consists of around 200-400 bones, with as many ribs attached.

Snakes have systematically-arranged organs. The first half of a snake's body (from its head) contains the main organs, like the brain and the heart. You can find the lungs and the liver after. The second half has organs like the bladder, small intestines, and kidneys.

Where They Live: A Snake's Habitat

Snakes live almost everywhere! They thrive mostly in tropical regions. You may see snakes under the ground, on trees, or even in the water.

Snakes are cold-blooded animals. Their body temperature changes depending on their surroundings. Sometimes, snakes need to bask in the sun to heat up, or crawl under a shade to cool down.

Snakes do not like the cold. If it is cold outside, snakes will feel cold too. A snake could stay inside a burrow to hibernate or seek warmer areas, like our houses.

Extraordinary Senses

Snakes have the five basic senses (sight, hearing, smell, taste, and touch) plus a sixth sense: heat reception. Though all snakes have these, not all snakes have the same quality of senses. The sharpness of each sense differs with each species because of different environmental and evolutionary factors.

One of the sharpest senses snakes have is their hearing. They hear using their jawbones to receive vibrations. In addition, their sense of touch is highly developed because their bodies are flooded with touch receptors. Furthermore, snakes have a powerful chemosensory device by combing the senses of smell and taste.

Lastly, snakes have extraordinary heat reception ability. They possess very sensitive organs called heat pits, which help snakes feel and seek heat. In some cases—pit vipers in particular—their heat pits are so sensitive that they can "see" differences in temperature.

Locomotion

Snakes move by slithering on the ground. They slither by contracting and relaxing their muscles. Sometimes, they use their scales to move. Currently, there are four known ways on how snakes slither.

Snakes move in a wavy motion by pushing against any surface. For tight spaces, however, snakes throw their bodies forward and backward to move. Snakes move sideways (called "sidewinding") to move on loose and slippery surfaces. Lastly, snakes move in a straight line by gripping scales to the ground and pushing forward.

Molting

Snakes change skins as they grow, a process called molting. Snakes molt because their skins do not grow with their bodies. Think of it as a person changing clothes that are too small for him.

When snakes are ready to molt, their eyes turn milky white, making them temporarily blinded. Clear scales, called spectacle scales, cover their entire eyes. To start shedding, snakes rub their noses against a rough surface, breaking the skin open. Slowly but surely, they slide out of their old skin.

Jaws and Fangs

Snakes have separate and flexible jaws, unlike ours. In fact, their jaws never dislocate! Muscles, tendons, and ligaments loosely connect the jaws. When eating, they can unhinge their jaws to swallow larger prey.

Snakes have four rows of upper teeth and two rows of lower teeth. Venomous snakes, however, are the only ones that have fangs. Fangs are sharp, hollow teeth that connect to a small sac in the snake's head behind its eyes. When snakes bite, their fangs can deliver venom, a poisonous liquid, to their prey.

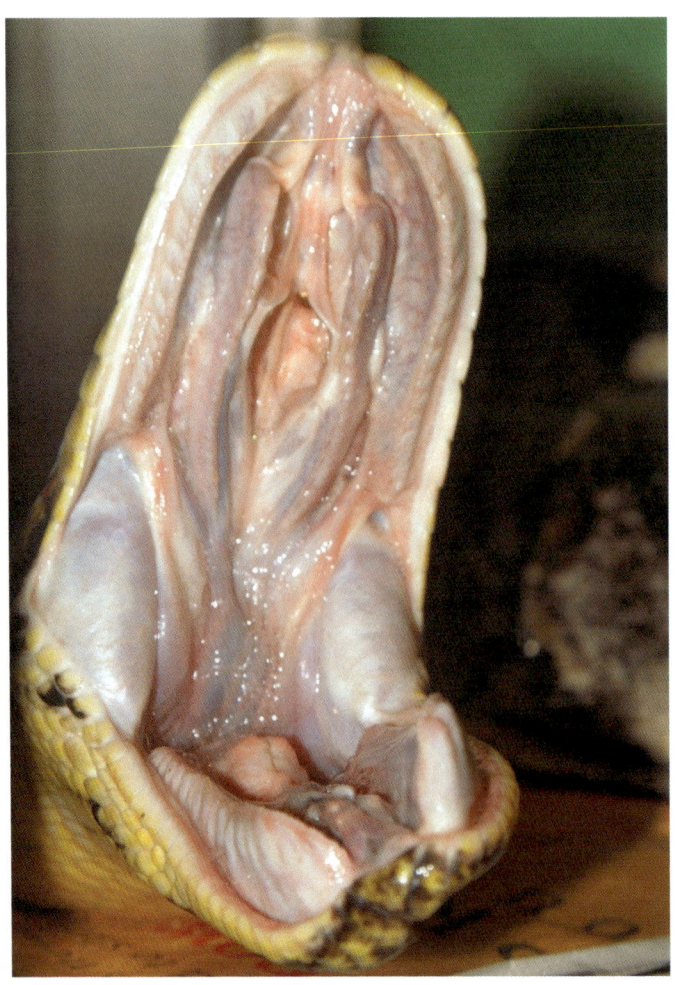

Feeding

Snakes are carnivores. They only eat meat. However, preferences over their diet differ for every snake. Some snakes like to eat small animals but some like to eat bigger ones for the long run.

Most snakes swallow their prey whole. In addition, most snakes constrict or strangle their prey to death before they eat them. On the other hand, venomous snakes like cobras and vipers use venom for hunting their prey.

Snakes are picky eaters. They know what they need to eat. The usual prey for a snake often represents the complete and balanced diet needed by that snake. For example, a mouse is a complete nutritional bundle for a rodent-eating snake.

Natural Defenses

Even with its scary fangs, snakes have their own predators. Their natural enemies include many kinds of birds, mammals, and even other snakes. Thus, snakes have their own ways to defend themselves.

Their colors help them blend with their surroundings. Sometimes, they can mimic things around them, like vines and dried leaves. Their color may also mimic other dangerous snakes. For example, the milk snake has almost the same pattern as a poisonous coral snake.

Snakes also have body parts that they use to intimidate predators. Rattles in rattlesnakes and the necks of cobras are just some. Furthermore, some species even hang their tongues out and play dead!

Mating Balls

Snakes usually mate during springtime, after they hibernate. Male snakes swarm females, creating a mating ball. These balls are not dance balls, but a battlefield where dozens of males compete to woo one female.

During the mating season, male snakes do not show aggression. They are solely focused on courting and mating. Sometimes, those few who successfully copulate prevent subsequent copulations from other male snakes.

Snakes and their Young

Snakes, according to how they give birth, can be classified into two groups: viviparous and oviparous. Viviparous refers to snakes that give birth to live young, like boas and green anacondas. Oviparous, on the other hand, indicates egg-laying snakes, like the coral snake and Burmese python.

Female snakes usually lay their eggs in a soft and warm place. Unlike bird eggs, snake eggs are soft and leathery. They are elastic enough to contain and protect baby snakes until the little snakes can survive on their own. Baby snakes do not get to see their mothers and have to survive on their own most of the time.

Mother snakes who give live birth actually hold the eggs inside their bodies. They do that to keep the baby snakes warm and safe from predators. When the eggs hatch inside, the mother gives birth to live baby snakes.

Anaconda

Anacondas are nonvenomous snakes of the Boa Constrictor family. They inhabit the Amazon jungles of South America. They live near lakes, rivers, and swamps. Anacondas can grow up to 6 meters long and weigh more than 140 kilograms.

Anacondas like to eat animals that they can find on land or in the water. They prey over frogs, fishes, ducks, birds, and turtles. If there were predators around, anacondas would rather slide quietly into the waters than confront them.

Black Mamba

One of the world's deadliest snakes is the black mamba. Black mambas are fast and venomous snakes. They inhabit the rocky hills and savannas of eastern and southern Africa.

Black mambas usually grow up to 8.2 feet in length. They have olive, brown, or gray scales. Usually shy, black mambas transform into deadly beasts when threatened. When they bite, they inject large amounts of venom with every strike.

Boa Constrictor

Boa constrictors are among the largest snakes in the world. Though they are nonpoisonous, they are just as deadly as other venomous snakes. It is because boa constrictors constrict their prey to death.

Boa constrictors thrive in hot and tropical areas, living on the ground and in trees. They usually eat birds, lizards, frogs, and small mammals. Sometimes, boas eat larger animals like monkeys, pigs, and deer.

Cobra

Cobras are extremely poisonous snakes. They thrive in hot, tropical areas in Australia, Africa, and Southern Asia. Cobras are excellent climbers and swimmers. Not only they live under the rocks and on trees, they also live near streams.

Cobras are famous for their threatening neck region, or the hood. They spread their hoods out when threatened or angry. They are also able to lift their heads high up the ground. These not only scare predators but also help them search for food.

Corn Snake

Corn snakes are nonvenomous snakes living in the southeastern parts of the United States. They usually live in places like forests and meadows, which can provide plenty of food for them. People keep them as pets where they help in controlling pests like their favorite prey – rodents.

Corn snakes can grow up to 2-3 feet in length. They are usually dark yellow or orange on color, depending on their habitat. Corn snakes are active during the day searching for food. If not, they rest on trees or under the rocks and bark.

Garter Snake

Garter snakes are common in the central United States and Canada. Their scales can have a variety of colors and markings. Usually 60-80 centimeters long, garter snakes can grow more than a meter long.

Garter snakes are small. Because of their size, they only prey on earthworms, fishes, frogs, leeches, and sometimes mice. They also have many predators like bears, birds, skunks, and raccoons.

Inland Taipan

Inland Taipans are some of the most venomous snakes in the world. They thrive in the semi-arid areas of central east Australia. Depending on the season, they can change their colors from brown, grey, and olive.

Inland Taipans feed on mammals. They like to eat rodents like the longhaired rats, plains rats, and even house mice. When hunting, they kill their prey with series of bites. They rapidly kill their prey by injecting extremely toxic venom into the prey's body.

Python

Pythons live near the equator, in Asia and Africa, where it is humid and warm. Some pythons live in cities and towns where food is abundant. Human activities destroy their natural habitats and their food sources.

Pythons are constrictors. Once their prey's heart stops beating, pythons swallow them whole. They usually feed on livestock (goats, chicken, pigs, and the like), lizards, antelopes, and monkeys.

Rattlesnake

Rattlesnakes are venomous snakes inhabiting deserts, mountains, and plains in the Western Hemisphere. They are known for their triangular or diamond-shaped heads and their rattles. Because of their rattles, they are the world's newest evolved snakes.

Rattlesnakes grow up to 4 feet in length. They usually feed on squirrels, rabbits, rodents, and small critters. Even with their venom, they are no match against kingsnakes.

Sea Snakes

Sea snakes are a species of snakes that inhabit the waters of the Indian and Pacific Oceans. Since they need air to breathe, they live in shallow waters. They can hold their breaths up to an hour!

Sea snakes have flat tails to swim. In addition, the flaps over their nostrils close to prevent inhaling water when they swim. They hunt under rocks and in reefs to find food. Sea snakes usually eat fish eggs, fishes, and eels.

Fun Facts about Snakes

1. Do you know that snake venom, despite being poisonous, can also be used as an antidote? Scientists process various snake venoms to produce a cure for the illnesses humans have today.

2. Some snakes can fly! The so-called flying snakes actually glide through the air. They flatten their ribs into a C-shape to trap air.

3. The skin of a snake reflects light. Very often, it looks wet, but it is actually dry.

4. The giant anaconda is the largest snake in the world, basing on its length-weight ratio. This species can grow up to 30 feet long and weigh half a ton!

5. You cannot find any snakes in Antarctica, Iceland, Ireland, Greenland, and New Zealand.

Comprehensive Questions

1. What do you call snakes that lay eggs?

2. Snakes only eat meat. This means that snakes are _____ animals.

3. Instead of limbs, snakes use what to slither?

4. Snakes have six senses. What sense do snakes use to seek heat?

5. A snake's skin doesn't grow with its body. What do you call the process where a snake changes its skin?

6. What species of snakes is famous for their threatening neck region, or the hood?

7. Snakes depend on their surroundings to change their body temperatures. This means that snakes are _____.

8. What species of snakes have rattles on their tails?

9. How many rows of teeth does a snake usually have?

10. What species of snakes is considered one of the most venomous snakes living in the semi-arid parts of central east Australia?

Comprehensive Answers

1. Answer: Oviparous

2. Carnivorous

3. Muscles

4. Heat Reception

5. Molting

6. Cobra

7. Coldblooded (Animals)

8. Rattlesnakes

9. Four (Rows)

10. Inland Taipan

More Pictures

Cobra

Coral-Snake

Isan-spitting-cobra-

Vine-snake-

Taiwan-Beauty-Snake-

Printed in Great Britain
by Amazon